NOVENA TO ST. CAJ

BIOGRAPHY AND POWERFUL PRAYERS TO PATRON OF WORK AND PROVISION

By

SIS LUCIA BRIANA

Copyright © All rights reserved @ SIS LUCIA BRIANA
2024

Table of contents

Biography of St. Cajetan

Chapter 1 : Day 1 Trust in Divine Providence

Chapter 2 : Day 2 Seeking Guidance and Wisdom

Chapter 3 : Day 3 Overcoming Financial Challenges

Chapter 4 : Day 4 Finding Employment

Chapter 5 : Day 5 Gratitude and Generosity

Chapter 6: Day 6 Perseverance and Faithfulness

Chapter 7 : Day 7 Protection and Peace

Chapter 8 : Day 8 Hope and Renewal

Chapter 9 : Day 9 Consecration to St. Cajetan

Conclusion

Introduction

St. Cajetan, a sixteenth-century Italian nobleman, abandoned his affluent lifestyle to dedicate his life to serving the poor and needy. Renowned for his unwavering faith and compassion, he founded the Clerics Regular, an order devoted to providing spiritual and material assistance to the marginalized. His life was marked by extraordinary acts of charity and a deep trust in Divine Providence.

Today, St. Cajetan is revered as the patron saint of work and provision. Countless individuals have turned to him in times of financial hardship, unemployment, and uncertainty. His intercession has been sought by those seeking guidance, support, and a renewed sense of hope.

The challenges of modern life often lead to anxieties about employment, financial stability, and material well-being. In these moments of doubt and fear, many find solace and strength in turning to St. Cajetan. As the patron saint of work and provision, he is believed to intercede on behalf of those who seek his help.

This novena invites you to embark on a nine- journey of prayer and reflection, drawing inspiration from the life and teachings of St. Cajetan. Through daily meditations and petitions, we will explore the themes of trust, gratitude, perseverance, and hope.

The Power of Novena Prayer

A novena is a nine-day period of focused prayer. It is a spiritual practice rooted in the belief that united prayer can be a powerful force for intercession. By joining together in prayer with countless others who venerate St. Cajetan, we can experience the transformative power of faith.

As we journey through this novena, let us open our hearts to the grace of God and the intercession of St. Cajetan. May this time of prayer deepen our trust in Divine Providence and equip us to face life's challenges with courage and resilience.

Brief History of St. Cajetan

Chapter 1

Saint Cajetan, a renowned Italian Catholic saint, was born on October 1, 1480, in Vicenza, a charming city in the Veneto region of northern Italy. During the Renaissance era, Vicenza was a thriving cultural and artistic hub, heavily influenced by the nearby city of Venice. This environment would later shape Cajetan's intellectual and spiritual pursuits.

Cajetan's family, the Thienes, were members of the nobility, holding significant social and economic status in Vicenza. His father, John Thiene, was a wealthy merchant, and his mother, Mary Porta, came from a respected family of Vicenza. The Thienes were devout Catholics, instilling in Cajetan a strong faith foundation from an early age.

Growing up in Vicenza, Cajetan was exposed to the city's rich cultural heritage, including its stunning architecture, art, and literature. He received a solid education, studying Latin, Greek, and philosophy, which laid the groundwork for his future academic and spiritual endeavors.

In his early years, Cajetan demonstrated a deep devotion to God and a strong sense of compassion for the poor and marginalized. These traits would become hallmarks of his later life and ministry, ultimately contributing to his sainthood.

As a young man, Saint Cajetan pursued higher education in various fields, cultivating his intellectual curiosity and spiritual growth. He enrolled in the University of Padua, a renowned institution of learning in northern Italy, where he studied law, philosophy, and theology. Cajetan's academic pursuits were marked by a desire to integrate his faith with his intellectual endeavors, laying the groundwork for his future vocation.

During his university years, Cajetan became increasingly devoted to practices of piety, which deepened his spiritual life and shaped his relationship with God. He was particularly drawn to the works of the early Church Fathers and the writings of Thomas Aquinas, whose teachings influenced his theological perspectives.

Cajetan's daily routine included regular prayer, meditation, and participation in the sacraments. He was especially devoted to the Eucharist, often spending hours in adoration and contemplation before the Blessed Sacrament. This intense focus on the Eucharist would later become a hallmark of his spiritual legacy.

In addition to his academic and spiritual pursuits, Cajetan also engaged in acts of charity and service, often visiting the sick, the poor, and the marginalized. These experiences instilled in him a profound sense of empathy and compassion, which would characterize his later ministry.

Through his early studies and practices of piety, Cajetan laid the foundation for a life of dedicated service to God and humanity. His commitment to intellectual and spiritual growth prepared him for the challenges and opportunities that lay ahead, ultimately leading him to found the Theatine Order and become a renowned saint of the Catholic Church.

Chapter 2

As Cajetan transitioned from adolescence to young adulthood, his commitment to piety only deepened, setting a remarkable example for his peers. Despite being surrounded by the temptations and distractions of university life, he remained steadfast in his devotion to God, cultivating a reputation as a model of virtue and spirituality.

Cajetan's youthful years were marked by an intense desire for spiritual growth, leading him to embrace various forms of asceticism and self-discipline. He practiced rigorous fasting, mortification, and penance, seeking to purify his soul and draw closer to God. These practices, though challenging, only served to strengthen his resolve and deepen his faith.

During this period, Cajetan also developed a strong affinity for the Blessed Virgin Mary, often seeking her intercession and guidance. He would frequently recite the Rosary, attend Marian devotions, and seek solace in her maternal care. This devotion to Mary would remain a constant throughout his life, influencing his spiritual direction and informing his later role as a founder of the Theatine Order.

Cajetan's exemplary piety did not go unnoticed by his contemporaries. Many young men, inspired by his witness, began to follow his example, embracing a more fervent and dedicated spiritual life. This ripple effect of Cajetan's influence would eventually contribute to a wider renewal of spirituality within the Church, as his message of piety, humility, and service resonated with an entire generation of Catholics.

Through his continued splendid example of piety, Cajetan demonstrated that genuine holiness is not solely the domain of the elderly or the cloistered, but can be cultivated by anyone, regardless of age or circumstance. His youthful years served as a testament to the power of faith and the human spirit, illuminating the path for all those seeking a deeper connection with God.

Following his academic pursuits in Padua, Cajetan remained in the city for several years, immersing himself in a life of piety and service. He became a familiar figure in the local churches, hospitals, and charitable institutions, where he devoted himself to prayer, preaching, and acts of mercy.

However, in 1506, Cajetan felt an interior calling to return to his native Vicenza, where he would embark on a new chapter in his spiritual journey. This decision marked a significant turning point in his life, as he began to discern a vocation to the ecclesiastical state.

Upon his return to Vicenza, Cajetan was ordained to the priesthood, a milestone that brought him immense joy and a deep sense of purpose. He threw himself into his priestly duties, celebrating Mass with reverence, preaching with conviction, and administering the sacraments with compassion.

As a priest, Cajetan became increasingly aware of the spiritual needs of his community, particularly the poor, the sick, and the marginalized. He spent countless hours visiting the afflicted, offering guidance and solace, and advocating for their welfare. His commitment to the ecclesiastical state had ignited a fire of charity within him, driving him to serve others with ever greater dedication.

In Vicenza, Cajetan also became acquainted with the works of St. Philip Neri, whose teachings on the importance of prayer, humility, and service resonated deeply with him. This influence would later shape Cajetan's own spiritual direction and inform the founding of the Theatine Order.

Through his embrace of the ecclesiastical state, Cajetan had discovered his true calling – a life of priestly service, marked by humility, compassion, and a unwavering commitment to the Gospel. This pivotal decision would propel him toward a future of remarkable spiritual fruitfulness, as he continued to respond to the Lord's invitation to serve.

Chapter 3

In 1509, Cajetan received an unexpected summons from Pope Julius II to present himself at the Vatican Palace in Rome. This invitation marked a significant turning point in Cajetan's life, as he was about to embark on a new chapter of service to the Church.

Upon his arrival in Rome, Cajetan was warmly received by the Pope, who had been impressed by his reputation for piety, intelligence, and administrative acumen. During their meeting, Pope Julius II expressed his desire to utilize Cajetan's skills in the service of the Holy See.

On December 13, 1509, the Pope appointed Cajetan as an Apostolic Notary, a prestigious position that entrusted him with the responsibility of authenticating official documents and conducting sensitive missions on behalf of the Pontiff. This appointment not only reflected Cajetan's growing reputation but also marked the beginning of his direct involvement in the central government of the Church.

As Apostolic Notary, Cajetan demonstrated exceptional diligence, integrity, and diplomatic skill, earning the respect and admiration of his peers. His expertise in canon law, combined with his linguistic proficiency in Latin, Italian, and Greek, made him an invaluable asset to the papal administration.

Cajetan's presence in Rome also afforded him opportunities to engage with prominent figures of the Renaissance, including artists, writers, and theologians. These encounters broadened his intellectual horizons, deepening his understanding of the complex issues facing the Church during this tumultuous period.

Through his appointment as Apostolic Notary, Cajetan had entered a new sphere of influence, one that would allow him to shape the course of Church history and pave the way for his future endeavors as a founder of the Theatine Order.

During his tenure as Apostolic Notary, Cajetan was dispatched to Venice on a sensitive diplomatic mission, aimed at resolving a longstanding dispute between the Republic of Venice and the Holy See. This assignment would prove to be a pivotal moment in Cajetan's life, as he demonstrated exceptional skill and dedication in serving the interests of both parties.

Upon his arrival in Venice, Cajetan was met with a complex web of political and ecclesiastical tensions. With his characteristic tact and diplomacy, he navigated the intricate landscape of Venetian politics, engaging in intense negotiations with the Doge and his advisors.

Through his tireless efforts, Cajetan succeeded in brokering a peace agreement between the Venetians and the Holy See, resolving a contentious issue that had threatened to escalate into a full-blown conflict. This achievement not only reflected Cajetan's exceptional diplomatic skills but also underscored his commitment to serving the greater good.

In addition to his diplomatic endeavors, Cajetan also rendered significant service to the Venetians through his spiritual ministry. He preached numerous sermons, administered the sacraments, and provided guidance to the faithful, earning a reputation as a compassionate and insightful spiritual director.

Cajetan's time in Venice also afforded him opportunities to engage with the city's vibrant cultural scene, where he encountered prominent artists, writers, and intellectuals. These encounters broadened his horizons, deepening his understanding of the complex interplay between faith, art, and culture.

Through his important services to the Venetians, Cajetan had demonstrated his value as a skilled diplomat, a compassionate spiritual guide, and a faithful servant of the Church. His accomplishments in Venice would serve as a testament to his remarkable versatility and dedication, paving the way for his future endeavors as a founder of the Theatine Order.

In 1516, Cajetan made a profound decision that would alter the trajectory of his life: he renounced his position as Protonotary Apostolic, a prestigious office that had brought him both influence and comfort. This selfless act was motivated by a deepening sense of spiritual calling, as Cajetan felt an insistent desire to dedicate himself more fully to the service of God.

With a sense of liberation and purpose, Cajetan began to prepare himself for the reception of Holy Orders. He understood that this step would enable him to offer the Holy Sacrifice of the Mass, a privilege he had long coveted. To prepare himself for this sacred responsibility, Cajetan embarked on a rigorous program of spiritual formation.

He devoted himself to intense prayer, immersing himself in the Scriptures, the writings of the Church Fathers, and the lives of the saints. Cajetan also engaged in fervent penance, seeking to purify his soul and conform himself more closely to the image of Christ.

Under the guidance of his spiritual director, Cajetan meticulously examined his conscience, seeking to identify areas for growth and improvement. He cultivated the virtues of humility, obedience, and charity, recognizing that these qualities were essential for a life of priestly service.

As he approached the day of his ordination, Cajetan's excitement and trepidation grew. He understood that the priesthood was not simply a profession or an office, but a sacramental reality that would configure him to Christ, the Eternal High Priest.

On September 24, 1516, Cajetan received the sacram of Holy Orders, being ordained to the priesthood by the Bishop of Venice. This moment marked the culmination of his spiritual journey thus far, as he was empowered to offer the Holy Sacrifice, administer the sacraments, and serve as a spiritual father to the faithful.

Through his renunciation of Protonotary and preparation for Holy Orders, Cajetan had demonstrated his unwavering commitment to the service of God and the Church. His priestly ordination would serve as a catalyst for his future endeavors, as he continued to respond to the Lord's invitation to serve with ever greater generosity and devotion.

Chapter 4

In 1517, Cajetan, now a priest, felt an interior prompting to establish a spiritual community in Rome, dedicated to the pursuit of holiness and the service of God. This inspiration led to the founding of the Oratory of Divine Love, a pioneering initiative that would become a beacon of spiritual renewal in the Eternal City.

The Oratory, initially composed of a small group of priests and laity, was characterized by an intense focus on prayer, penance, and charity. Cajetan, as its founder and spiritual director, encouraged members to embrace a life of evangelical perfection, marked by detachment, humility, and a passionate love for God.

As the Oratory flourished, Cajetan received extraordinary graces from our Lord, which profoundly deepened his spiritual life and informed his leadership. He experienced frequent visions, ecstasies, and mystical communications, through which God revealed to him the secrets of His heart and the needs of His Church.

One remarkable grace granted to Cajetan was the ability to discern the interior state of those who approached him for spiritual guidance. This charism enabled him to offer personalized direction, tailored to the unique needs and struggles of each individual.

Another extraordinary favor was the gift of tears, which Cajetan received during his intense prayers and devotions. This physical manifestation of his interior sorrow and love for God became a hallmark of his spiritual life, symbolizing his profound compassion for the suffering Christ and his desire for redemption.

Through the Oratory of Divine Love, Cajetan created a sanctuary of spiritual growth, where men and women could gather to seek God, support one another, and serve the Church. As its founder, he embodied the values of humility, charity, and zeal, inspiring countless individuals to follow in his footsteps and embrace a life of radical discipleship.

In 1518, Cajetan received news that his mother, Mary Porta, was gravely ill in Vicenza. Without hesitation, he returned to his hometown to be at her side during her final moments. This filial devotion was characteristic of Cajetan's compassionate nature, as he had always prioritized the needs of others, even in the midst of his own spiritual pursuits.

Upon his arrival in Vicenza, Cajetan was met with the sorrowful reality of his mother's impending passing. He spent countless hours by her bedside, offering emotional support, spiritual guidance, and tender care. As Mary Porta drew closer to eternity, Cajetan prayed fervently for her soul, seeking to ensure her peaceful transition into eternal life.

Following his mother's passing, Cajetan remained in Vicenza, where he became aware of the Oratory of St. Jerome, a spiritual community that had fallen into disarray. Recognizing an opportunity to revitalize this dormant institution, Cajetan undertook the task of reforming the Oratory, infusing it with the same spirit of renewal that had characterized his work in Rome.

Under Cajetan's guidance, the Oratory of St. Jerome flourished, attracting men and women seeking spiritual growth, prayer, and community. He established a rigorous program of devotions, including daily Mass, recitation of the Divine Office, and frequent confession. Cajetan also introduced the practice of spiritual direction, offering one-on-one guidance to members seeking a deeper understanding of their faith.

Through his reform of the Oratory of St. Jerome, Cajetan demonstrated his commitment to spreading the values of the Oratory of Divine Love, which he had founded in Rome. By transplanting this spiritual model to Vicenza, he aimed to create a network of like-minded communities, united in their pursuit of holiness and service to the Church.

In 1520, Cajetan's compassion and zeal for serving the suffering led him to establish a hospital for incurables in Vicenza. This pioneering institution, dedicated to caring for those afflicted with terminal illnesses, reflected Cajetan's commitment to embracing the most vulnerable members of society.

The hospital, which quickly gained a reputation for its exceptional care and spiritual support, became a testament to Cajetan's innovative approach to charity and his ability to mobilize resources for the greater good. By providing a safe haven for the incurably ill, Cajetan not only alleviated their physical suffering but also offered them spiritual comfort and companionship.

Following the successful establishment of the hospital in Vicenza, Cajetan expanded his ministry to Verona, a nearby city in northern Italy. There, he replicated his model of spiritual and charitable service, preaching, teaching, and caring for the sick and the poor.

In Verona, Cajetan's presence sparked a renewed sense of spiritual fervor, as he drew people from all walks of life to his sermons, devotions, and acts of charity. His selflessness, kindness, and unwavering dedication to serving others inspired countless individuals to reevaluate their priorities and embrace a more authentic Christian lifestyle.

Through his tireless efforts in Vicenza and Verona, Cajetan demonstrated that his vision for a more compassionate and spiritually vibrant society knew no geographical bounds. As his reputation grew, so did the scope of his influence, inspiring a wider circle of admirers and emulators to follow in his footsteps.

In 1522, Cajetan arrived in Venice, a city renowned for its beauty, wealth, and cultural sophistication. Yet, beneath its dazzling facade, Venice grappled with profound spiritual and social challenges. It was here that Cajetan would undertake some of the most remarkable works of his ministry, leaving an indelible mark on the city and its inhabitants.

Upon his arrival, Cajetan was struck by the stark contrast between the city's opulence and the widespread poverty, immorality, and spiritual apathy that afflicted its citizens. Undaunted, he threw himself into a whirlwind of apostolic activity, preaching, teaching, and serving the poor, the sick, and the marginalized.

One of Cajetan's most notable achievements in Venice was the establishment of a monte di pieta, a charitable institution providing low-interest loans to the poor, thereby liberating them from the clutches of usury. This innovative initiative not only alleviated economic hardship but also fostered a sense of community and social responsibility.

Cajetan also founded a hospital for incurables in Venice, replicating the model he had successfully implemented in Vicenza. This hospital, dedicated to caring for those afflicted with terminal illnesses, became a beacon of hope and compassion, reflecting Cajetan's unwavering commitment to serving the most vulnerable members of society.

Furthermore, Cajetan's preaching and teaching in Venice had a profound impact on the city's spiritual landscape. He drew vast crowds to his sermons, delivering messages that were both uncompromising and compassionate, calling his listeners to repentance, conversion, and a deeper embrace of their faith.

Through his extraordinary works in Venice, Cajetan demonstrated his remarkable ability to adapt his ministry to the unique needs of each context, while remaining faithful to his core values of compassion, humility, and service. His legacy in Venice would endure long after his departure, inspiring future generations to follow in his footsteps.

Chapter 5

In the early 16th century, Cajetan, a renowned spiritual leader and founder of the Theatine Order, maintained a profound and lasting impact on the lives of numerous individuals through his extensive correspondence. Among his notable exchanges were those with Sister Laura Mignani and Bartholomew Stella, both natives of Brescia.

Sister Laura Mignani, a member of the Order of St. Clare, was distinguished by her extraordinary piety, humility, and mystical experiences. Her letters to Cajetan, characterized by spiritual insight and vulnerability, reveal a deep trust in his guidance and a desire for spiritual growth. Through her correspondence, Sister Laura sought Cajetan's counsel on matters of faith, discernment, and spiritual direction.

Bartholomew Stella, a layman from Brescia, was equally devoted to Cajetan, seeking his guidance on matters of faith, morality, and spiritual direction. Their correspondence, marked by warmth, sincerity, and mutual respect, testifies to the profound impact of Cajetan's ministry on the lives of those who encountered him.

The letters exchanged between Cajetan, Sister Laura, and Bartholomew provide a unique glimpse into the spiritual landscape of 16th-century Italy. They reveal a complex web of spiritual seeking, discernment, and growth, as these individuals navigated the challenges of their faith journeys.

Through his correspondence with Sister Laura and Bartholomew, Cajetan demonstrated his remarkable ability to adapt his guidance to the unique needs and circumstances of each individual. His letters, filled with wisdom, compassion, and spiritual insight, offered practical advice, encouragement, and support, helping his correspondents navigate the complexities of their spiritual journeys.

In 1524, Cajetan, driven by his ardent devotion to the Eucharist, introduced the Exposition of the Blessed Sacrament in Venice. This innovative practice, which involved the public display of the consecrated host, aimed to foster a deeper reverence for the Real Presence and promote spiritual growth among the faithful.

To promote this initiative, Cajetan penned a letter to his niece, Elizabeth, a testament to his commitment to sharing his spiritual vision with others. In this letter, he eloquently expressed his passion for the Eucharist, emphasizing its centrality in Christian life and its power to transform individuals and communities.

Cajetan's letter to Elizabeth serves as a spiritual testament, offering insights into his own devotion to the Eucharist and his desire to share this gift with others. Through his words, we glimpse the fervor and conviction that drove him to establish the Exposition of the Blessed Sacrament, a practice that would become a hallmark of his spiritual legacy.

The Exposition of the Blessed Sacrament, as introduced by Cajetan, involved the solemn display of the consecrated host in a monstrance, accompanied by prayer, hymns, and meditation. This practice, which continues to be observed in many Catholic churches today, provides a powerful opportunity for spiritual reflection, worship, and community building.

Through his establishment of the Exposition of the Blessed Sacrament in Venice, Cajetan demonstrated his innovative approach to spiritual leadership, his commitment to fostering deeper devotion to the Eucharist, and his passion for sharing the riches of the Christian faith with others. His letter to Elizabeth stands as a testament to the enduring power of his spiritual vision, inspiring future generations to embrace the beauty and mystery of the Eucharist.

In the early 16th century, Cajetan, a visionary and innovative spiritual leader, conceived the idea of establishing a new religious order, the Order of Regular Clergy, also known as the Theatines. This groundbreaking initiative aimed to address the pressing needs of the Church and society, while providing a unique model of clerical life and ministry.

Cajetan's thoughts on the foundation of his new order were shaped by his profound understanding of the Church's challenges and his desire to revitalize its spiritual and pastoral life. He envisioned an order that would combine the contemplative and active dimensions of religious life, fostering a deep sense of spirituality, community, and apostolic zeal among its members.

Key Principles:

1. Spiritual Renewal: Cajetan sought to create an order that would prioritize spiritual growth, prayer, and devotion, recognizing that a deep interior life was essential for effective ministry.

2. Apostolic Flexibility: He envisioned an order that would be adaptable and responsive to the changing needs of the Church and society, embracing innovative approaches to evangelization and pastoral care.

3. **Community Life:** Cajetan emphasized the importance of community and fraternal life, recognizing that a supportive and prayerful environment was crucial for the spiritual and emotional well-being of his clergy.

4. **Clerical Reform:** He aimed to establish an order that would embody the highest standards of clerical integrity, simplicity, and dedication, providing a model for reform within the Church.

5. **Missionary Zeal:** Cajetan instilled in his order a passion for missionary work, encouraging his members to engage in evangelization, education, and charitable activities.

By founding the Order of Regular Clergy, Cajetan sought to create a dynamic and responsive community of priests and brothers who would embody the values of spiritual renewal, apostolic flexibility, community life, clerical reform, and missionary zeal. His vision continues to inspire and guide the Theatine Order to this day, offering a powerful model for religious life and ministry in the modern world.

Chapter 6

In 1527, Cajetan departed Venice, returning to his hometown of Vicenza, where a devastating outbreak of the plague had claimed numerous lives. Undaunted by the risks, Cajetan dedicated himself to serving the afflicted, providing spiritual comfort, and caring for the sick.

During this period of intense ministry, Cajetan experienced a profound vision, which deepened his understanding of God's will and his own vocation. This mystical encounter reinforced his commitment to serving the Lord and His people, particularly in times of crisis.

As Cajetan navigated the challenges of the plague, he began to reevaluate his relationship with material wealth. Recognizing the transience of earthly riches, he made his first renouncement of his inheritance, embracing a life of simplicity and detachment.

Following his experiences in Vicenza, Cajetan embarked on a pilgrimage to Loreto, a renowned Marian shrine. This journey allowed him to express his devotion to the Mother of God and seek her intercession for the afflicted. His visit to Loreto marked a significant milestone in his spiritual journey, as he continued to discern God's will for his life.

Through his selfless service during the plague, his profound vision, his renouncement of riches, and his pilgrimage to Loreto, Cajetan demonstrated his unwavering dedication to his faith and his unshakeable commitment to serving others. These experiences would shape his future endeavors, as he continued to respond to the Lord's call with courage, humility, and generosity.

In the early 16th century, Cajetan, a visionary and innovative spiritual leader, embarked on a groundbreaking endeavor: the foundation of a new religious institute, the Order of Regular Clergy, also known as the Theatines. This pioneering initiative aimed to address the pressing needs of the Church and society, while providing a unique model of clerical life and ministry.

Cajetan's vision for his new institute was shared by two like-minded individuals, Boniface da Colle and John Peter Carafa, who would become his first companions and collaborators. Their stories, intertwined with Cajetan's, form a rich tapestry of spiritual seeking, friendship, and apostolic zeal.

Boniface da Colle:

- Born in Vicenza, Italy, Boniface was a member of the noble da Colle family.

- He was drawn to Cajetan's vision and joined him in his apostolic endeavors.

- Boniface brought his expertise in canon law and theology to the fledgling institute.

- He played a crucial role in shaping the order's early development and governance.

John Peter Carafa:

- Born in Naples, Italy, John Peter was a member of the noble Carafa family.

- He was a skilled theologian and canonist, who shared Cajetan's passion for reform.

- John Peter joined Cajetan and Boniface in their apostolic endeavors, bringing his expertise to the foundation.

- He would later become a prominent leader within the Theatine Order, serving as its second superior general.

Together, Cajetan, Boniface, and John Peter formed a formidable team, united in their commitment to spiritual renewal, apostolic flexibility, and clerical reform. Their collaboration laid the foundation for the Theatine Order, which would become a beacon of hope and reform within the Church. Through their shared vision and endeavors, they demonstrated the power of friendship and collaboration in shaping a new era of spiritual growth and apostolic zeal.

Chapter 7

In the early 16th century, a young and devout priest named Paul Consilieri became an integral part of the burgeoning Theatine community. His life and ministry were deeply intertwined with those of Cajetan and Carafa, the founders of the Order of Regular Clergy.

Paul Consilieri:

- Born in Vicenza, Italy, Paul was drawn to the priesthood at a young age.

- He was introduced to Cajetan and Carafa, and quickly became a close friend and confidant.

- Paul shared their passion for spiritual renewal and clerical reform, and joined their apostolic endeavors.

- He brought his own unique gifts and talents to the community, including a deep understanding of scripture and a talent for preaching.

Intimacy with Cajetan and Carafa:

- Paul's relationship with Cajetan was marked by a deep spiritual affinity and trust.

- He often served as Cajetan's secretary and confidant, and was privy to his innermost thoughts and feelings.

- Paul's friendship with Carafa was equally close, and the two men frequently collaborated on theological and pastoral projects.

- Together, the three men formed a powerful triumvirate, united in their commitment to reforming the Church and promoting spiritual growth.

Contributions to the Theatine Community:

- Paul played a key role in shaping the Theatine community's spiritual practices and devotions.

- He was instrumental in developing the order's constitutions and governance structures.

- Paul's preaching and teaching helped to spread the Theatine message, attracting new members and supporters to the community.

Through his intimacy with Cajetan and Carafa, Paul Consilieri became an indispensable part of the Theatine founding narrative. His life and ministry serve as a testament to the power of friendship and collaboration in shaping a new era of spiritual growth and apostolic zeal.

Cajetan's innovative approach to religious life and his determination to establish a new order, the Theatines, were met with significant opposition and difficulties. Despite his unwavering commitment to his vision, he faced numerous challenges from both within and outside the Church.

Opposition from the Church:

- Cajetan's emphasis on apostolic simplicity, poverty, and flexibility was seen as a threat to traditional monastic structures and practices.

- Some Church leaders viewed his approach as too radical, fearing it would lead to instability and disorder.

- Cajetan faced resistance from those who preferred a more rigid and formalized approach to religious life.

Difficulties from Within:

- Cajetan's own companions and followers sometimes struggled to understand and embrace his vision.

- Internal conflicts and disagreements arose, testing Cajetan's leadership and resolve.

- The demands of establishing a new order, combined with the intense spiritual and physical demands of his own ministry, took a toll on Cajetan's health and well-being.

Overcoming Opposition and Difficulties:

- Cajetan remained steadfast in his commitment to his vision, drawing strength from his deep faith and spiritual convictions.

- He engaged in open and respectful dialogue with his critics, seeking to address their concerns and win them over to his perspective.

- Through his own example of humility, simplicity, and apostolic zeal, Cajetan inspired his companions and followers to persevere in the face of adversity.

- He sought guidance from trusted spiritual advisors and mentors, including his friend and confidant, Gian Pietro Carafa.

Through his unwavering determination and creative problem-solving, Cajetan overcame the numerous challenges that threatened to derail his vision. His ability to navigate opposition and difficulties ultimately strengthened his resolve and paved the way for the successful establishment of the Theatine Order.

Chapter 8

Cajetan's innovative approach to religious life and his determination to establish a new order, the Theatines, required him to present compelling arguments to gain approval from the Church authorities. His persuasive reasoning and prophetic insights ultimately won over the hearts and minds of those who would shape the future of his institute.

Arguments for Approval:

- Cajetan emphasized the need for a more apostolic and flexible approach to religious life, one that would allow for greater engagement with the world and more effective evangelization.

- He argued that his institute would provide a unique opportunity for spiritual growth and development, combining the best elements of monastic and apostolic traditions.

- Cajetan presented a clear and compelling vision for his order, outlining its mission, values, and practices in a way that resonated with the Church's own priorities and concerns.

Approval and Recognition:

- Cajetan's arguments and vision won the approval of Pope Clement VII, who recognized the potential of the Theatine Order to revitalize the Church and promote spiritual renewal.

- The Pope granted Cajetan's institute official recognition, paving the way for its establishment and growth.

Cajetan's success in obtaining approval for his institute was seen as a testament to his prophetic insight and his ability to discern the will of God.

Prophecy Regarding the Institute:

- Cajetan received a prophetic vision regarding the future of his institute, foreseeing its growth and impact on the Church.

- He saw the Theatine Order as a beacon of hope and reform, shining brightly in a world filled with darkness and uncertainty.

- Cajetan's prophecy was seen as a confirmation of his institute's divine origin and purpose, inspiring his companions and followers to embrace their mission with renewed passion and commitment.

Through his persuasive arguments and prophetic insights, Cajetan secured the approval and recognition his institute needed to flourish. His vision and leadership continue to inspire generations of Theatines, shaping the course of their history and guiding their mission to this day.

On a momentous day in 1524, Cajetan and his companions gathered at the iconic St. Peter's Basilica in Rome to make their solemn profession, a public declaration of their commitment to the Theatine Order. This milestone event marked a significant turning point in the history of the institute, as its founders and early members formally dedicated themselves to a life of apostolic service and spiritual renewal.

Preparations for the Profession:

- Cajetan and his companions spent weeks in intense spiritual preparation, engaging in prayer, fasting, and meditation to purify their hearts and minds.

- They sought guidance from their spiritual directors and confessors, ensuring that their decision to make solemn profession was made with discernment and clarity.

- The group also worked tirelessly to complete the necessary paperwork and formalities, obtaining the required permissions and approvals from Church authorities.

The Profession Ceremony:

- On the appointed day, Cajetan and his companions processed into St. Peter's Basilica, accompanied by a solemn liturgical procession.

- The ceremony was officiated by a high-ranking Church official, who led the group through the ritual of profession.

- Cajetan and his companions individually professed their vows of poverty, chastity, and obedience, committing themselves to a life of apostolic service and spiritual growth.

Significance of the Profession:

- The solemn profession marked a definitive step in the establishment of the Theatine Order, formalizing its existence and mission.

- Cajetan's leadership and vision were reaffirmed, as he and his companions publicly dedicated themselves to the institute's core values and principles.

- The event sent a powerful message to the Church and the world, demonstrating the group's commitment to reform, renewal, and service.

Aftermath and Celebration:

- Following the profession ceremony, Cajetan and his companions celebrated with a festive meal and joyful festivities.

- The event was attended by dignitaries, friends, and supporters of the Theatine Order, who came to witness and honor the group's commitment.

- The solemn profession at St. Peter's marked a new beginning for the Theatine Order, as its members embarked on a journey of apostolic service, spiritual growth, and reform within the Church.

Chapter 9

In the early 16th century, a spiritual revival swept through Rome, led by visionary figures such as Cajetan and his companions. At the heart of this movement were two iconic locations: Campo Marzio and Monte Pincio. These sites became synonymous with a new form of preaching, evangelical poverty, and Franciscan reform, inspiring a generation of spiritual seekers and reformers.

Campo Marzio:

- This bustling Roman square became a hub for open-air preaching, as Cajetan and his companions shared their message of spiritual renewal and reform with the masses.

- Their preaching style was characterized by simplicity, passion, and a focus on the Gospel message, resonating deeply with the common people.

- Campo Marzio emerged as a symbol of the Theatine Order's commitment to evangelization and apostolic service.

Monte Pincio:

- This picturesque hill overlooking Rome became a retreat for Cajetan and his companions, a place for spiritual reflection and contemplation.

- Inspired by the Franciscan ideal of evangelical poverty, they embraced a simple and austere lifestyle, renouncing material possessions and worldly comforts.

- Monte Pincio represented the Theatine Order's dedication to spiritual growth, prayer, and community life.

New Form of Preaching:

- Cajetan and his companions pioneered a new approach to preaching, emphasizing the importance of personal experience, emotional connection, and spiritual authenticity.

- Their message focused on the transformative power of the Gospel, calling listeners to a deeper conversion and commitment to Christ.

- This innovative style of preaching captivated audiences and inspired a new generation of preachers and evangelists.

Evangelical Poverty:

- The Theatine Order embraced evangelical poverty as a core value, renouncing material wealth and embracing simplicity and austerity.

- This commitment to poverty allowed them to identify with the marginalized and oppressed, sharing in their struggles and ministering to their needs.

- Evangelical poverty became a hallmark of the Theatine charism, inspiring a life of detachment, generosity, and service.

Franciscan Reform:

- The Theatine Order drew inspiration from the Franciscan tradition, embracing its emphasis on poverty, simplicity, and apostolic service.

- Cajetan and his companions sought to reform the Church from within, promoting a more authentic and evangelical approach to religious life.

- Their Franciscan-inspired reform movement helped shape the contours of Catholic reform in the 16th century, influencing generations of spiritual leaders and reformers.

In the early 16th century, Rome faced a series of ominous warnings and prophetic signs indicating an impending disaster. These celestial chastisements and prophetic utterances foretold the coming evil that would soon engulf the city, culminating in the devastating Sack of Rome in 1527.

Warnings from Heaven:

- Astronomical phenomena, such as comets and eclipses, were seen as harbingers of doom, signaling God's displeasure with the city's corruption and sin.

- Prophets and visionaries, including Catholic mystics, foretold the coming destruction, urging repentance and reform.

- Earthquakes and natural disasters struck the city, serving as a warning of the impending calamity.

The Coming Evil:

- The rise of Charles V, Holy Roman Emperor, and his powerful armies posed a significant threat to Rome's stability and independence.

- The city's corruption, nepotism, and moral decay created an environment ripe for divine chastisement.

- The warning signs and prophetic utterances were ignored or dismissed by the city's leaders, leading to a lack of preparedness for the impending disaster.

The Sacking of Rome:

- On May 6, 1527, Imperial troops, largely composed of Lutheran mercenaries, breached the city walls, unleashing a wave of destruction and chaos.

- The city was pillaged, and its inhabitants suffered greatly, with many killed, tortured, or displaced.

- The Sack of Rome marked a turning point in the city's history, leading to a period of rebuilding and reform.

The warnings and prophetic signs that preceded the Sack of Rome served as a call to repentance and reform, urging the city's leaders and inhabitants to address their spiritual and moral shortcomings. The devastating consequences of ignoring these warnings continue to serve as a reminder of the importance of heeding divine guidance and embracing reform.

During the tumultuous Sack of Rome in 1527, Cajetan and his companions stood firm in their faith, exemplifying extraordinary courage and spiritual resilience. As the city burned and chaos reigned, they clung to their convictions, inspiring others to do the same.

They trusted in God's providence, believing that He was in control even amidst the devastation. They saw the sack as a divine chastisement, an opportunity for spiritual growth and renewal. Despite the peril, Cajetan and his companions continued their ministry, tending to the wounded, comforting the afflicted, and preaching hope.

They faced danger with courage, relying on their faith to sustain them. Cajetan's leadership during the sack inspired his companions and others to remain steadfast in their faith. His example of calm and trust in God helped to mitigate the panic and despair that gripped the city.

They turned to prayer, seeking solace and strength in their devotion to God. Their prayers and hymns became a source of comfort and inspiration for those around them. The faith of Cajetan and his companions during the sack of Rome served as a powerful witness to the transformative power of belief.

Their unwavering commitment to God inspired others to re-examine their own faith and seek a deeper connection with the divine. In the midst of unimaginable destruction, Cajetan and his companions stood as beacons of hope, their faith shining brightly for all to see. Their example continues to inspire generations, a testament to the enduring power of trust, courage, and devotion.

Cajetan and his companions endured immense physical and emotional suffering during the Sack of Rome in 1527. Despite their own tribulations, they continued to minister to the afflicted and comfort the sorrowful.

They were subjected to physical violence and mistreatment by the invading troops, and suffered from hunger, thirst, and exposure as they struggled to survive amidst the chaos. Many of them fell ill, contracting diseases that spread rapidly in the devastated city.

The companions witnessed unimaginable atrocities, including the slaughter of innocent civilians and the desecration of sacred sites. They grappled with feelings of helplessness, despair, and frustration, as they struggled to come to terms with the scale of the destruction. Cajetan himself was deeply troubled by the suffering of his people, feeling the weight of responsibility as a spiritual leader. They faced intense spiritual struggles, wrestling with doubts and fears about God's presence and providence. They grappled with the seeming silence of God, as they cried out for reliefand deliverance

Cajetan and his companions had to confront their own limitations and weaknesses, relying on their faith to sustain them. Despite these immense sufferings, they remained steadfast in their commitment to God and to one another. Their example of courage, resilience, and compassion continues to inspire generations, a testament to the transformative power of faith in the face of adversity.

Cajetan and his companions, exhausted and devastated by the Sack of Rome, made the difficult decision to leave the city and journey to Venice. They sought refuge in the northern Italian city, hoping to find safety and solace after the trauma they experienced.

As they traveled, they reflected on the events that had transpired, struggling to come to terms with the destruction and chaos they witnessed. They grappled with feelings of loss and grief, but also found comfort in their shared experience and their commitment to one another.

Upon arriving in Venice, they were met with kindness and generosity by the local population. They found solace in the city's beauty and tranquility, and began to rebuild their lives and their community. Cajetan and his companions continued their ministry, preaching and serving the poor and marginalized.

Despite the challenges they faced, they remained steadfast in their faith and their commitment to one another. They found strength in their shared experiences and their devotion to God, and slowly began to heal and rebuild. Their journey to Venice marked a new chapter in their lives, one of hope and renewal after the devastation of Rome.

Following their arrival in Venice, Cajetan and his companions established a new foundation, the House of St. Nicholas da Tolentino. In recognition of his leadership and spiritual guidance, Cajetan was elected Superior of the community.

Under his direction, the house flourished, becoming a center of spiritual growth, apostolic service, and charitable works. Cajetan's daily life was marked by a deep commitment to prayer, contemplation, and service to others.

He received numerous graces from Heaven, including profound spiritual insights, mystical experiences, and the gift of healing. These blessings enabled him to guide his companions and serve the people of Venice with greater effectiveness.

Cajetan's works in Venice included:

- Establishing a hospital for the sick and the poor

- Founding a school for the education of children

- Providing spiritual direction and counseling to those in need

- Preaching and teaching the Gospel message

Through his tireless efforts, Cajetan transformed the House of St. Nicholas da Tolentino into a beacon of hope and a symbol of God's love in the heart of Venice. His legacy continues to inspire generations, a testament to the power of faith, compassion, and dedication to serving others.

Chapter 10

In the early 16th century, Venice faced an unprecedented crisis as famine and pestilence swept through the city, leaving death and destruction in their wake. Amidst this chaos, Cajetan, then Superior of the House of St. Nicholas da Tolentino, emerged as a beacon of hope, exemplifying superhuman charity and compassion.

A severe famine hit Venice, causing widespread suffering and desperation among the population. Food was scarce, and the poor and vulnerable suffered the most. Cajetan sprang into action, using his leadership and resources to alleviate the suffering.

He organized food distribution, ensuring that the hungry were fed, and established soup kitchens to provide sustenance for the needy. Cajetan personally visited the afflicted, offering comfort, spiritual guidance, and material support.

Just as the famine began to subside, a deadly pestilence broke out in Venice, claiming countless lives and spreading fear and panic. Cajetan, undaunted by the danger, continued his tireless work, caring for the sick, comforting the grieving, and burying the dead.

His selfless efforts inspired others to join him, and soon a team of volunteers worked alongside him, providing medical care, food, and shelter to those affected.

Cajetan's response to the famine and pestilence was characterized by extraordinary charity, compassion, and generosity. He:

- Sold his own possessions to fund relief efforts
- Went into debt to provide for the needy
- Risked his own life to care for the sick and dying
- Offered spiritual guidance and comfort to the afflicted

Cajetan's superhuman charity earned him the admiration and gratitude of the people of Venice, who saw in him a living example of Christ's love and compassion.

Cajetan's selfless efforts during the famine and pestilence left an indelible mark on the city of Venice. His legacy of compassion and charity continues to inspire generations, reminding us of the transformative power of selfless love and service to others.

Cajetan played a pivotal role in the establishment of the Congregation of Somasca, a religious order dedicated to the care of orphans, the sick, and the poor. His contributions to the institution were instrumental in shaping its mission, values, and legacy.

In 1534, Cajetan, along with his companions, founded the Congregation of Somasca in Somasca, Italy. The congregation's primary objective was to provide care and support to marginalized communities, including orphans, the sick, and the poor.

Cajetan's vision for the congregation was rooted in his deep commitment to serving the most vulnerable members of society. He believed that by providing education, healthcare, and spiritual guidance, the congregation could empower individuals to break the cycle of poverty and improve their socio-economic status.

Cajetan served as the first Superior General of the Congregation of Somasca, providing leadership and guidance to its members. He established the congregation's rules and regulations, which emphasized the importance of humility, simplicity, and charity.

Under his leadership, the congregation flourished, expanding its reach to various parts of Italy and beyond. Cajetan's charisma and spiritual guidance attracted numerous vocations, and the congregation became known for its dedication to serving the poor and marginalized.

Cajetan's spiritual legacy continued to shape the Congregation of Somasca long after his death. His emphasis on compassion, empathy, and selfless service inspired generations of Somascans to follow in his footsteps.

The congregation's commitment to education, healthcare, and social justice remains a testament to Cajetan's vision and leadership. Today, the Congregation of Somasca continues to serve vulnerable communities worldwide, upholding the values of charity, humility, and simplicity that Cajetan instilled in its founders.

Cajetan's extraordinary gift for conversion was exemplified in his encounter with B. Giovanni Marinoni, a young nobleman from Venice. Marinoni, who was known for his worldly and dissolute lifestyle, was transformed by Cajetan's guidance and became a devoted follower of God.

He met Marinoni while preaching in Venice. Initially, Marinoni was skeptical and even mocking of Cajetan's message. However, Cajetan's kindness, compassion, and unwavering commitment to his faith eventually won Marinoni over.

He took Marinoni under his wing, providing spiritual guidance and mentorship. He introduced Marinoni to the teachings of the Gospel and encouraged him to develop a personal relationship with God.

Through Cajetan's guidance, Marinoni underwent a profound transformation. He renounced his worldly ways and embraced a life of prayer, penance, and service to others.

Marinoni's conversion was so remarkable that he eventually became a priest and later a bishop. He credited Cajetan for his transformation and remained deeply devoted to him.

Cajetan's legacy continues to inspire generations, demonstrating the power of faith, compassion, and mentorship in transforming lives. Marinoni's story serves as a testament to Cajetan's remarkable ability to touch hearts and minds, and his unwavering commitment to spreading the Gospel message.

Cajetan's influence on Marinoni's life was a testament to his extraordinary gift for conversion, and his ability to bring people to God through his words, actions, and example. Marinoni's transformation was a miracle that continues to inspire and motivate people to this day.

He sent Carafa to Verona at the entreaty of Monsignor Giberti, and afterwards Bonifacio da Colle, to found a House of his Order. He later went there in person, where he reconciled the Church with her Bishop.

Cajetan's desire to spread his Order and promote unity in the Church led him to send his trusted companions, Carafa and Bonifacio da Colle, to Verona. They were tasked with establishing a new House and promoting reconciliation between the Church and its Bishop.

Upon their arrival, they faced numerous challenges, but Cajetan's guidance and support enabled them to overcome obstacles and achieve their goals. The House was successfully established, and the Church was reconciled with its Bishop.

His personal involvement in the mission was instrumental in its success. He traveled to Verona, where he employed his exceptional diplomatic skills to bring about a lasting reconciliation. His presence and influence helped to soothe tensions and foster a spirit of cooperation.

Through this mission, Cajetan demonstrated his unwavering commitment to his Order's principles and his dedication to promoting unity within the Church. His efforts in Verona served as a testament to his remarkable leadership and his ability to bring people together in the pursuit of a common goal.

He undertook a significant reform of the Divine Office, aiming to revitalize the liturgical practices of his Order. His efforts focused on promoting a more authentic and fervent celebration of the liturgy, emphasizing the importance of prayer and contemplation.

As his reform gained momentum, Cajetan was summoned to Naples by the local authorities, who sought his expertise in implementing similar reforms within their own diocese. This invitation presented Cajetan with an opportunity to expand his influence and share his vision with a broader audience.

In Naples, Cajetan worked tirelessly to promote his reform, engaging with local clergy and religious leaders to foster a deeper understanding of the liturgy and its significance. His efforts were met with enthusiasm and support, as many recognized the value of his proposals.

Through his work in Naples, Cajetan's reform of the Divine Office gained further momentum, spreading to other regions and inspiring a renewed focus on liturgical renewal. His dedication to this cause left a lasting impact on the Church, shaping the course of liturgical development for generations to come.

His commitment to reform was driven by his passion for authenticity and fervor in worship. He believed that a renewed emphasis on the Divine Office would revitalize the spiritual lives of clergy and laity alike, fostering a deeper connection with God and a more profound sense of community.

As Cajetan's influence extended beyond his own Order, his reform of the Divine Office became a beacon of hope for those seeking to revitalize their spiritual practices. His work in Naples represented a significant milestone in this journey, marking a major step forward in the spread of his reform and its enduring impact on the Church.

Cajetan's journey to Naples was a significant event in his life, marked by a sense of purpose and duty. He traveled to Naples in response to a summons from the local authorities, who sought his expertise in reforming the liturgical practices of their diocese.

Chapter 11

Cajetan and his companions were received with great enthusiasm and warmth upon their arrival in Naples. The local clergy and religious leaders, who had been eagerly awaiting their arrival, welcomed them with open arms.

Despite the fanfare and attention, Cajetan remained humble and grounded, preferring to focus on the task at hand rather than basking in the praise of others. His admirable constancy in the face of adoration and admiration was a testament to his unwavering commitment to his mission.

As Cajetan and his companions settled into their new surroundings, they were struck by the beauty and vibrancy of the city. They were particularly drawn to the stunning architecture and rich cultural heritage of Naples, which seemed to embody the very spirit of Italy.

However, Cajetan's focus remained fixed on his mission to reform the liturgical practices of the Church. He spent many hours engaging with local clergy and religious leaders, sharing his vision and expertise with them.

Throughout his time in Naples, Cajetan demonstrated remarkable constancy and perseverance. Despite facing numerous challenges and setbacks, he remained steadfast in his commitment to his mission, never wavering in his dedication to the cause.

Cajetan's admirable constancy inspired countless individuals in Naples, who were drawn to his unwavering passion and conviction. His presence in the city left a lasting impact, shaping the course of liturgical reform and spiritual renewal for generations to come.

Through his remarkable example, Cajetan showed that true greatness is not measured by external accolades or recognition, but by the depth of one's commitment to their values and principles. His legacy continues to inspire and motivate individuals to this day, a testament to the enduring power of his admirable constancy.

Cajetan's time in Naples was marked by numerous remarkable events, including a extraordinary miracle of healing that took place at St. Maria del Popolo and St. Maria della Stalletta.

It was here that Cajetan encountered a young girl who was afflicted with a severe and debilitating illness. The girl's condition was so dire that she was unable to move or respond to her surroundings, and her family had lost all hope of her recovery.

Cajetan, moved by the girl's suffering and her family's despair, prayed fervently for her healing. He placed his hands upon her and invoked the power of God, asking that she be restored to full health.

As he prayed, a miraculous transformation took place. The girl's eyes, which had been closed and unresponsive, suddenly opened, and she looked up at Cajetan with a gaze full of wonder and gratitude.

Her body, which had been paralyzed and still, began to stir, and she slowly sat up, looking around in awe at her surroundings. Her family, who had been watching in amazement, erupted into tears of joy, thanking Cajetan and God for the miraculous healing.

The news of this miracle spread quickly throughout Naples, and soon people were flocking to Cajetan, seeking his intercession and prayers. Cajetan, however, remained humble and grounded, attributing the miracle to God's power and mercy, rather than his own.

This miracle was just one of many that took place during Cajetan's time in Naples, and it served as a testament to his remarkable faith and his ability to tap into the power of God. It also deepened his reputation as a holy and compassionate man, and cemented his place in the hearts of the people.

Cajetan's commitment to reform and renewal extended beyond his own Order, as he worked tirelessly to promote the reform of two convents, the Dominicanesses and the Poor Clares.

The Dominicanesses, a community of Dominican nuns, had fallen into a state of spiritual laxity and worldly attachment. Cajetan, recognizing the need for reform, worked closely with the nuns to revive their commitment to prayer, penance, and service.

Through his guidance and encouragement, the Dominicanesses began to embrace a more austere and contemplative way of life, renouncing worldly attachments and focusing on their spiritual growth.

Similarly, the Poor Clares, a community of Franciscan nuns, had also strayed from their founding ideals. Cajetan worked with the Poor Clares to restore their commitment to poverty, simplicity, and devotion to God.

He encouraged them to embrace a more radical poverty, renouncing unnecessary possessions and focusing on their spiritual development. He also promoted a deeper commitment to prayer and contemplation, encouraging the nuns to spend more time in quiet reflection and communion with God.

Through his efforts, both convents underwent a profound transformation, returning to their founding ideals and embracing a more authentic and fervent spiritual life.

Cajetan's promotion of reform in these convents was marked by his characteristic humility, compassion, and wisdom. He worked collaboratively with the nuns, listening to their concerns and offering guidance and support.

His efforts bore fruit, as the Dominicanesses and Poor Clares flourished under his guidance, becoming beacons of spiritual renewal and reform in the Church. Cajetan's legacy continued to inspire and motivate generations of religious women, shaping the course of their spiritual development and commitment to God.

Cajetan's ministry was marked by a remarkable gift for converting penitents, bringing countless individuals back to the fold of the Church. His extraordinary ability to touch hearts and minds was rooted in his deep understanding of human nature, his compassion, and his unwavering commitment to the Gospel.

Cajetan's approach to conversion was characterized by empathy, kindness, and patience. He took the time to listen to each individual's story, understanding their struggles, fears, and doubts. He then shared the message of God's love and mercy, presenting the Gospel in a way that was both compelling and accessible.

Through his words and example, Cajetan helped penitents to see the error of their ways and to desire a deeper relationship with God. He encouraged them to embrace a life of prayer, penance, and service, and to seek forgiveness for their sins.

Cajetan's conversion of penitents was not limited to individuals, but also extended to entire communities. He worked tirelessly to bring about reconciliation and healing in families, neighborhoods, and cities, promoting a culture of forgiveness and understanding.

One of the most remarkable aspects of Cajetan's conversion of penitents was his ability to bring people back to the sacraments. He encouraged individuals to seek out Confession, to receive Holy Communion, and to participate in the life of the Church.

Through his efforts, countless penitents experienced a profound transformation, turning away from sin and embracing a life of holiness. Cajetan's legacy as a converter of penitents continues to inspire and motivate individuals to this day, a testament to the enduring power of his ministry.

Cajetan, known for his extraordinary gifts of discernment and prophecy, once shared a remarkable prediction with Padre Carafa, a fellow priest who would later become a Cardinal. At the time, Carafa was a young and ambitious priest, eager to make a name for himself in the Church.

Cajetan, sensing Carafa's potential and ambition, took him aside and shared a prophecy that would shape the course of his life. He told Carafa that he would one day be elected Cardinal, but warned him that this honor would come with great responsibility and challenge.

Cajetan's prophecy was not only a prediction of Carafa's future, but also a call to humility and service. He cautioned Carafa against the dangers of pride and ambition, urging him to remain grounded in his faith and committed to the service of others.

Cajetan's prophecy to Carafa also contained guidance on how to rule a religious community. He advised Carafa to lead with humility, compassion, and wisdom, always prioritizing the needs of others above his own.

He emphasized the importance of creating a sense of family and community within the religious order, where members felt supported, encouraged, and loved. He encouraged Carafa to foster a spirit of collaboration and shared responsibility, where each member felt valued and empowered to contribute.

His method of ruling a religious community was rooted in his own experience as a founder and leader of the Theatines. He knew that effective leadership required a deep understanding of human nature, a strong sense of compassion, and a commitment to serving others.

Through his prophecy and guidance, Cajetan helped shape Carafa's approach to leadership, inspiring him to become a wise and compassionate leader who would go on to make a profound impact on the Church.

Cajetan and his companions had been residing at St. Maria della Stalletta, a small church in Naples, for some time. However, they felt a strong desire to move to a more central location, where they could better serve the community and spread their message.

After much prayer and discernment, Cajetan and his companions decided to exchange St. Maria della Stalletta for St. Paolo Maggiore, a larger and more prominent church in the heart of Naples.

The exchange was not without its challenges, as St. Paolo Maggiore was in a state of disrepair and had been neglected for many years. However, Cajetan and his companions saw this as an opportunity to restore the church to its former glory and make it a beacon of hope and spiritual renewal in the community.

With the help of some generous donors and skilled craftsmen, Cajetan and his companions set about restoring St. Paolo Maggiore. They worked tirelessly to repair the damaged structures, clean the church, and adorn it with beautiful artwork and furnishings.

As the restoration progressed, the church began to take on a new life. The once-neglected building was transformed into a vibrant and welcoming space, filled with the sounds of prayer, music, and laughter.

Cajetan and his companions also established a thriving community at St. Paolo Maggiore, attracting many young men who were drawn to their way of life. They established a school, a hospital, and other charitable institutions, making the church a hub of activity and service in the city.

Through their hard work and dedication, Cajetan and his companions restored St. Paolo Maggiore to its former glory, creating a beautiful and vibrant space that would serve as a testament to their faith and commitment for generations to come.

Chapter 12

During his time in Naples, Cajetan faced a significant challenge in the form of heresy. A group of individuals, influenced by the teachings of the Protestant Reformation, had begun to spread their erroneous beliefs throughout the city.

Cajetan, recognizing the danger that heresy posed to the souls of the faithful, sprang into action. He preached tirelessly against the heretics, using his powerful oratory skills to expose the errors of their teachings and to defend the Catholic faith.

Despite facing opposition and persecution from the heretics, Cajetan remained steadfast in his commitment to the truth. He worked closely with the Archbishop of Naples and other Church leaders to develop a comprehensive plan to combat the spread of heresy.

Through his efforts, Cajetan was able to prevent the heresy from taking hold in Naples. He converted many of those who had been led astray, bringing them back to the fold of the Church.

Cajetan's success in saving Naples from heresy was due in large part to his extraordinary gifts as a preacher and his deep understanding of the Catholic faith. He was able to present the teachings of the Church in a clear and compelling way, making it easy for people to understand and embrace the truth.

In addition to his preaching, Cajetan also worked to promote devotion to the Blessed Sacrament and to encourage the faithful to receive Holy Communion frequently. He believed that a strong devotion to the Eucharist was essential for maintaining the faith and resisting the influence of heresy.

Through his tireless efforts, Cajetan saved Naples from the scourge of heresy, preserving the faith of the people and ensuring the continued vitality of the Church in the city. His legacy as a champion of orthodoxy and a defender of the faith has endured for centuries, inspiring generations of Catholics to remain faithful to the teachings of the Church.

After his successful mission in Naples, Cajetan returned to Venice and Verona, where he continued to preach, teach, and guide his spiritual sons.

In Venice, Cajetan was greeted with great enthusiasm by the people, who had grown to love and respect him during his previous time in the city. He resumed his preaching and teaching, drawing large crowds and inspiring many to deepen their faith.

He also spent time in Verona, where he worked to strengthen the Theatine community and promote the reform of the Church. He preached in the city's churches and cathedrals, and met with the local clergy and laity to encourage them in their spiritual journeys.

During his time in Venice and Verona, Cajetan continued to emphasize the importance of prayer, penance, and service to others. He encouraged his followers to live simple lives, detached from worldly possessions and desires, and to focus on growing in holiness and virtue.

His return to Venice and Verona was also marked by a renewed emphasis on the importance of education and intellectual pursuits. He believed that a well-educated clergy and laity were essential for the reform of the Church and the spread of the Gospel.

To this end, Cajetan worked to establish schools and libraries in both cities, where young men could study theology, philosophy, and the arts. He also encouraged the establishment of confraternities and other lay organizations, which would provide a framework for Catholics to come together and support one another in their spiritual journeys.

Through his tireless efforts, Cajetan helped to create a vibrant and dynamic Catholic community in Venice and Verona, one that would continue to thrive long after his death. His legacy as a preacher, teacher, and reformer has endured for centuries, inspiring countless Catholics to follow in his footsteps and strive for holiness.

After his successful mission in Venice and Verona, Cajetan returned to Naples, where he was greeted with great enthusiasm by the people. He had been away for several years, and his return was seen as a blessing by the faithful.

Upon his return, Cajetan resumed his preaching and teaching, drawing large crowds and inspiring many to deepen their faith. He also spent time with his spiritual sons, guiding them and encouraging them in their spiritual journeys.

Cajetan's return to Naples was marked by a renewed emphasis on the importance of prayer and penance. He encouraged the faithful to turn away from sin and to seek forgiveness through the sacraments. He also promoted devotion to the Blessed Sacrament and encouraged the faithful to receive Holy Communion frequently.

During his time in Naples, Cajetan also worked to strengthen the Theatine community, establishing new houses and recruiting new members. He also worked to promote the reform of the Church, encouraging the clergy and laity to work together to bring about a renewal of faith and practice.

One of the most notable events of Cajetan's return to Naples was his establishment of a new hospital, dedicated to caring for the sick and the poor. This hospital, which became known as the "Hospital of the Incurables," was a testament to Cajetan's commitment to serving the most vulnerable members of society.

Through his tireless efforts, Cajetan helped to create a vibrant and dynamic Catholic community in Naples, one that would continue to thrive long after his death. His legacy as a preacher, teacher, and reformer has endured for centuries, inspiring countless Catholics to follow in his footsteps and strive for holiness.

Cajetan's return to Naples was also marked by a deepening of his spiritual life. He spent long hours in prayer, seeking guidance and strength from God. He also practiced intense penance, seeking to purify himself and prepare for the challenges that lay ahead.

Chapter 13

As Cajetan's life drew to a close, he remained committed to his mission of serving God and the Church. Despite his advanced age and frail health, he continued to preach, teach, and guide his spiritual sons.

One of Cajetan's last actions was to convene a gathering of his Theatine community, where he exhorted them to remain faithful to their calling and to continue their work of reforming the Church. He also appointed a successor to lead the community after his death, ensuring that his legacy would continue.

He also spent time in prayer and contemplation, preparing himself for the end of his life. He received the sacraments, including Holy Communion and the Anointing of the Sick, and was surrounded by his spiritual sons and friends.

In his final days, Cajetan's thoughts turned to his beloved Naples, the city where he had spent so much of his life and ministry. He expressed his gratitude to God for the opportunity to serve the people of Naples and prayed for their continued spiritual growth and renewal.

On August 7, 1547, Cajetan passed away, surrounded by his community and friends. His death was met with widespread mourning, as the people of Naples and beyond recognized the loss of a truly holy and dedicated servant of God.

Cajetan's last actions were a testament to his unwavering commitment to his faith and his mission. Even in his final days, he remained focused on serving God and inspiring others to do the same. His legacy continues to inspire and motivate Catholics to this day, a reminder of the power of faith, prayer, and service to others.

As Cajetan's life drew to a close, he continued to demonstrate his perfect obedience to God's will. Despite his physical weakness and suffering, he remained steadfast in his commitment to his faith and his community.

One of the last proofs of Cajetan's perfect obedience was his acceptance of his own mortality. He knew that his time on earth was coming to an end, and he welcomed death as a transition to eternal life with God.

Cajetan's obedience was also evident in his willingness to suffer. He had always believed that suffering was a means of purifying the soul and drawing closer to God, and he embraced his own suffering with courage and resignation.

In his final days, Cajetan was unable to move or speak, but he continued to express his obedience through his silence and his acceptance of his condition. He was a powerful example of surrender to God's will, even in the face of great physical and emotional pain.

The last proofs of Cajetan's perfect obedience also included his devotion to the Blessed Sacrament. He had always had a deep love for the Eucharist, and in his final days, he was able to receive Holy Communion one last time.

Cajetan's perfect obedience was also evident in his forgiveness of others. He had always taught that forgiveness was essential for spiritual growth, and he practiced what he preached, forgiving those who had wronged him and asking for forgiveness from those he had wronged.

Through his last proofs of perfect obedience, Cajetan left a powerful legacy for his community and for the Church. He showed that obedience to God's will is the key to true freedom and happiness, and that surrender to God's plan is the ultimate expression of love and devotion.

Cajetan's fatal illness was a prolonged and debilitating condition that eventually took his life. The exact nature of his illness is not certain, but it is believed to have been a combination of factors, including:

1. Exhaustion: Cajetan's tireless work and travels had taken a significant toll on his physical health. He had spent years preaching, teaching, and guiding his spiritual sons, often going without rest or relaxation.

2. Dysentery: Cajetan had suffered from dysentery, a bacterial infection that causes diarrhea, abdominal pain, and fever. This illness had weakened his body and made him more susceptible to other health problems.

3. Pneumonia: Some accounts suggest that Cajetan may have contracted pneumonia, a serious infection that inflames the lungs and can be life-threatening.

4. Heart condition: Cajetan may have had an underlying heart condition, which could have contributed to his decline.

The cause of Cajetan's fatal illness was likely a combination of these factors, exacerbated by his advanced age and years of physical and emotional strain.

Despite his illness, Cajetan remained committed to his faith and his community, continuing to preach and teach until his body could no longer sustain him. His death on August 7, 1547, was a testament to his unwavering dedication to God and his unshakeable trust in divine providence.

Cajetan's fatal illness and its cause serve as a reminder of the human frailty and the importance of caring for one's physical and spiritual health. His legacy continues to inspire and motivate Catholics to this day, a testament to the power of faith, obedience, and selfless service to others.

Cajetan's death on August 7, 1547, was a significant event in the history of the Catholic Church. His passing was mourned by his spiritual sons, the Theatine community, and the people of Naples, who had grown to love and respect him.

After his death, Cajetan's body was prepared for burial according to the customs of the time. He was dressed in his Theatine habit and placed in a simple wooden coffin.

The funeral procession was led by the Archbishop of Naples, accompanied by the Theatine community, clergy, and laity. The procession wound its way through the streets of Naples, stopping at various churches and shrines along the way.

Cajetan was buried in the church of San Paolo Maggiore, which he had helped to restore and where he had spent many hours in prayer. His sepulcher was a simple stone tomb, adorned with a marble slab bearing his name and the inscription: "Cajetan, Founder of the Theatines."

Over time, Cajetan's sepulcher became a place of pilgrimage for those seeking his intercession and guidance. Many miracles were reported to have occurred at his tomb, and his reputation as a saint and a powerful intercessor grew.

In 1671, Cajetan's remains were transferred to a new tomb in the same church, designed by the famous architect, Cosimo Fanzago. The new tomb was a magnificent marble structure, adorned with intricate carvings and statues of angels and saints.

Today, Cajetan's sepulcher remains a place of devotion and pilgrimage, a testament to his enduring legacy and his continued influence on the lives of Catholics around the world.

The inscription on his tomb reads: "Cajetan, Founder of the Theatines, Apostle of Naples, and Saint of the Catholic Church. His body rests here, but his spirit lives on in the hearts of those who seek his guidance and intercession."

Beatification:

- The process of beatification for St. Cajetan began in 1623, just 76 years after his death.

- In 1629, Pope Urban VIII declared Cajetan "Venerable", recognizing his heroic virtues.

- On October 8, 1630, Cajetan was beatified by Pope Urban VIII, declaring him "Blessed".

Canonization:

- The process of canonization began soon after Cajetan's beatification.

- In 1669, Pope Clement IX declared Cajetan's martyrdom and miracles to be authentic.

- On April 12, 1671, Pope Clement X canonized Cajetan, declaring him a saint.

- The canonization ceremony took place in Rome, with many dignitaries and Theatine priests in attendance.

Recognition of Cajetan's Sanctity:

- Cajetan's beatification and canonization were recognition of his extraordinary virtues, miracles, and devotion to God.

- His canonization was a testament to his influence on the Catholic Church and his role as a model for Christian living.

Celebration of Cajetan's Canonization:

- The canonization was celebrated with great fanfare in Naples, Rome, and other cities.

- The Theatine community celebrated with special Masses, processions, and festivities.

- Cajetan's canonization was seen as a triumph for the Theatine order and a recognition of their founder's sanctity.

The Sanctity of Cajetan

Cajetan's sanctity was evident throughout his life, marked by his extraordinary virtues, miracles, and devotion to God. His commitment to prayer, penance, and service to others was unwavering, inspiring countless individuals to follow in his footsteps.

Virtues:

- **Humility:** Cajetan's humility was legendary. He refused to seek honors or recognition, instead preferring to serve others in obscurity.

- **Charity:** Cajetan's love for the poor, sick, and marginalized was boundless. He spent countless hours serving them, often going without food or sleep.

- **Purity:** Cajetan's purity of heart and intention was remarkable. He remained chaste and detached from worldly desires, focusing solely on God.

Miracles:

- Healing of the sick: Cajetan was known to have healed many sick individuals through his prayers and intercession.

- Multiplication of food: During a famine in Naples, Cajetan prayed for food to be multiplied, and bread and other essentials were miraculously provided.

- Protection from danger: Cajetan protected his community from harm on several occasions, including a devastating earthquake in Naples.

Chapter 1

Day 1

Trust in Divine Providence

Opening Prayers

In the name of the Father, and of the Son, and of the Holy Spirit. Amen.

Act of Contrition

O my God, I am heartily sorry for having offended You, and I detest all my sins because of Your love for me. I resolve with Your help to confess my sins, to do penance, and to amend my life. Amen.

Theme and Reflection

We begin our novena to St. Cajetan by focusing on trust in Divine Providence. Like St. Cajetan, we are called to place our complete confidence in God's care and provision. Let us reflect on the importance of surrendering our anxieties and trusting in God's perfect plan for our lives.

Meditation and Prayer Requests

As we meditate on St. Cajetan's life, let us ask for his intercession in the following areas:

Deepening our trust in God

Overcoming anxiety and worry

Accepting God's will with peace

A spirit of surrender

Scripture Reading

Matthew 6:25-34 "Therefore I tell you, do not worry about your life, what you will eat or drink; or about your body, what you will wear. Is not life more important than food, and the body more important than clothes? Look at the birds of the air; they do not sow or reap or store away in barns, and yet your heavenly Father feeds them. Are you not much more valuable than they? Can any one of you by worrying add a single hour to your life? And why do you worry about clothes? See how the lilies of the field grow. They do not labor or spin. Yet I tell you that not even Solomon in all his splendor was dressed like one of these. If that is how God clothes the grass of the field, which is here today and tomorrow is thrown into the### Prayer for Employment and Overcoming Financial Difficulties O Saint Cajetan, patron of work and provision, help us to cultivate a deep trust in Divine Providence. As we face the challenges of employment and financial difficulties, remind us that God is our provider and protector. Grant us the peace and confidence that comes from knowing we are in God's hands. Help us to surrender our anxieties and to trust in your intercession. Amen.

Closing Prayers

Our Father, who art in heaven, hallowed be thy name; thy kingdom come; thy will be done; on earth as it is in heaven. Give us this day our daily bread. And forgive us our trespasses, as we forgive those who trespass against us. And lead us not into temptation, but deliver us from evil. For thine is the kingdom, and the power, and the glory, for ever and ever. Amen.

Hail Mary, full of grace, the Lord is with thee. Blessed art thou amongst women, and blessed is the fruit of thy womb, Jesus. Holy Mary, Mother of God, pray for us sinners, now and at the hour of our death. Amen.

Hail, holy Queen, Mother of mercy, hail, our life, our sweetness and our hope. To thee do we cry, poor banished children of Eve: to thee do we send up our sighs, mourning and weeping in this vale of tears. Turn then, mostgracious Advocate, thine eyes of mercy toward us, and after this our exile, show unto us the blessed fruit of thy womb, Jesus. O clement, O loving, O sweet Virgin Mary! Pray for us, O holy Mother of God, that we may be made worthy of the promises of Christ. Amen.

Glory be to the Father, and to the Son, and to the Holy Spirit. As it was in the beginning, is now, and ever shall be, world without end. Amen.

Prayer for Employment and Overcoming Financial Difficulties

O Saint Cajetan, patron of work and provision, we turn to you with humble hearts, seeking your powerful intercession. We come before you burdened by the weight of unemployment and financial hardship. We implore your guidance and assistance as we navigate these challenging times.

Grant us the strength and perseverance to seek employment with diligence and determination. Open doors of opportunity before us, and may our skills and talents find fruitful employment. Fill our hearts with hope as we search for work that is both fulfilling and financially rewarding.

We ask for your blessing upon our financial situation. Help us to manage our resources wisely and to overcome our debts. Protect us from reckless spending and instill in us a spirit of contentment and gratitude. May your divine providence guide us towards financial stability and abundance.

We trust in your compassionate heart and unwavering love. Intercede for us before the throne of God, and grant us the grace to overcome these challenges. Amen.

St. Cajetan, pray for us.

In the name of the Father, and of the Son, and of the Holy Spirit. Amen.

Chapter 2

Day 2

Seeking Guidance and Wisdom

Opening prayers

Act of Contrition

O my God, I am heartily sorry for having offended You, and I detest all my sins because of Your love for me. I resolve with Your help to confess my sins, to do penance, and to amend my life. Amen.

Theme and Reflection

Today, we turn our hearts to St. Cajetan, seeking his intercession for guidance and wisdom. In a world often filled with uncertainty, we long for clarity and discernment. Let us reflect on the importance of seeking God's will in all things.

Meditation and Prayer Requests

As we meditate on St. Cajetan's life, let us ask for his intercession in the following areas:

Discernment in making important life decisions

Wisdom to overcome challenges

Guidance in finding our true purpose

Strength to trust in God's plan

Scripture Reading

Proverbs 3:5-6 Trust in the Lord with all your heart, and do not rely on your own insight. In all your ways acknowledge him, and he will direct your paths.

Closing Prayers

Our Father, who art in heaven, hallowed be thy name; thy kingdom come; thy will be done; on earth as it is in heaven. Give us this day our daily bread. And forgive us our trespasses, as we forgive those who trespass against us. And lead us not into temptation, but deliver us from evil. For thine is the kingdom, and the power, and the glory, for ever and ever. Amen.

Hail Mary, full of grace, the Lord is with thee. Blessed art thou amongst women, and blessed is the fruit of thy womb, Jesus. Holy Mary, Mother of God, pray for us sinners, now and at the hour of our death. Amen.

Hail, holy Queen, Mother of mercy, hail, our life, our sweetness and our hope. To thee do we cry, poor banished children of Eve: to thee do we send up our sighs, mourning and weeping in this vale of tears. Turn then, mostgracious Advocate, thine eyes of mercy toward us, and after this our exile, show unto us the blessed fruit of thy womb, Jesus. O clement, O loving, O sweet Virgin Mary! Pray for us, O holy Mother of God, that we may be made worthy of the promises of Christ. Amen.

Glory be to the Father, and to the Son, and to the Holy Spirit. As it was in the beginning, is now, and ever shall be, world without end. Amen.

Prayer for Employment and Overcoming Financial Difficulties

O Saint Cajetan, patron of work and provision, we turn to you in our time of need. Guide us towards opportunities that align with our talents and passions. Help us to overcome obstacles in our job search and to find employment that is both fulfilling and financially rewarding. Intercede for us as we face financial challenges, granting us the wisdom to manage our resources wisely and the strength to trust in God's providence. Amen.

St. Cajetan, pray for us.

In the name of the Father, and of the Son, and of the Holy Spirit. Amen.

Chapter 3

Day 3

Overcoming Financial Challenges

Opening Prayers

In the name of the Father, and of the Son, and of the Holy Spirit. Amen.

Act of Contrition

O my God, I am heartily sorry for having offended You, and I detest all my sins because of Your love for me. I resolve with Your help to confess my sins, to do penance, and to amend my life. Amen.

Theme and Reflection

Today, we turn our attention to the financial challenges that many face. St. Cajetan, known for his compassion for the poor, understands our struggles. Let us place our trust in Divine Providence and seek His guidance as we navigate these difficult times.

Meditation and Prayer Requests

As we meditate on St. Cajetan's life, let us ask for his intercession in the following areas:

Relief from financial burdens

Wisdom in managing finances

Strength to resist materialism

A generous spirit

Scripture Reading

Matthew 6:33 But seek first the kingdom of God and his righteousness, and all these things will be added to you.

Closing Prayers

Our Father, who art in heaven, hallowed be thy name; thy kingdom come; thy will be done; on earth as it is in heaven. Give us this day our daily bread. And forgive us our trespasses, as we forgive those who trespass against us. And lead us not into temptation, but deliver us from evil. For thine is the kingdom, and the power, and the glory, for ever and ever. Amen.

Hail Mary, full of grace, the Lord is with thee. Blessed art thou amongst women, and blessed is the fruit of thy womb, Jesus. Holy Mary, Mother of God, pray for us sinners, now and at the hour of our death. Amen.

Hail, holy Queen, Mother of mercy, hail, our life, our sweetness and our hope. To thee do we cry, poor banished children of Eve: to thee do we send up our sighs, mourning and weeping in this vale of tears. Turn then, mostgracious Advocate, thine eyes of mercy toward us, and after this our exile, show unto us the blessed fruit of thy womb, Jesus. O clement, O loving, O sweet Virgin Mary! Pray for us, O holy Mother of God, that we may be made worthy of the promises of Christ. Amen.

Glory be to the Father, and to the Son, and to the Holy Spirit. As it was in the beginning, is now, and ever shall be, world without end. Amen.

Prayer for Employment and Overcoming Financial Difficulties

O Saint Cajetan, patron of work and provision, we come to you burdened by financial worries. We ask for your intercession to alleviate our financial burdens and provide for our needs. Help us to develop a spirit of gratitude and contentment, trusting in God's providence. Grant us the wisdom to make sound financial decisions and the strength to overcome our challenges. Amen.

St. Cajetan, pray for us.

In the name of the Father, and of the Son, and of the Holy Spirit. Amen.

Chapter 4

Day 4

Finding Employment

Opening Prayers

In the name of the Father, and of the Son, and of the Holy Spirit. Amen.

Act of Contrition

O my God, I am heartily sorry for having offended You, and I detest all my sins because of Your love for me. I resolve with Your help to confess my sins, to do penance, and to amend my life. Amen.

Theme and Reflection

Today, we focus our prayers on finding employment. St. Cajetan, understanding the challenges of the job market, is our intercessor. Let us trust in God's providence as we seek work that aligns with our talents and passions.

Meditation and Prayer Requests

As we meditate on St. Cajetan's life, let us ask for his intercession in the following areas:

Success in job searches

Confidence in interviews

Patience during the job-seeking process

A fulfilling career

Scripture Reading

Jeremiah 29:11 "For I know the plans I have for you," declares the Lord, "plans to prosper you and not to harm you, plans to give you hope and a future."

Closing Prayers

Our Father, who art in heaven, hallowed be thy name; thy kingdom come; thy will be done; on earth as it is in heaven. Give us this day our daily bread. And forgive us our trespasses, as we forgive those who trespass against us. And lead us not into temptation, but deliver us from evil. For thine is the kingdom, and the power, and the glory, for ever and ever. Amen.

Hail Mary, full of grace, the Lord is with thee. Blessed art thou amongst women, and blessed is the fruit of thy womb, Jesus. Holy Mary, Mother of God, pray for us sinners, now and at the hour of our death. Amen.

Hail, holy Queen, Mother of mercy, hail, our life, our sweetness and our hope. To thee do we cry, poor banished children of Eve: to thee do we send up our sighs, mourning and weeping in this vale of tears. Turn then, mostgracious Advocate, thine eyes of mercy toward us, and after this our exile, show unto us the blessed fruit of thy womb, Jesus. O clement, O loving, O sweet Virgin Mary! Pray for us, O holy Mother of God, that we may be made worthy of the promises of Christ. Amen.

Glory be to the Father, and to the Son, and to the Holy Spirit. As it was in the beginning, is now, and ever shall be, world without end. Amen.

Prayer for Employment and Overcoming Financial Difficulties

O Saint Cajetan, patron of work and provision, we turn to you with hope and trust as we seek employment. Guide us in our job search, helping us to discover opportunities that match our skills and aspirations. Grant us the confidence and perseverance needed to succeed in interviews. May we find work that is both fulfilling and financially rewarding. Amen.

St. Cajetan, pray for us.

In the name of the Father, and of the Son, and of the Holy Spirit. Amen.

Chapter 5

Day 5

Gratitude and Generosity

Opening Prayers

In the name of the Father, and of the Son, and of the Holy Spirit. Amen.

Act of Contrition

O my God, I am heartily sorry for having offended You, and I detest all my sins because of Your love for me. I resolve with Your help to confess my sins, to do penance, and to amend my life. Amen.

Theme and Reflection

Today, we focus on gratitude and generosity. Even amidst challenges, we can find blessings to be thankful for. Let us cultivate a heart of gratitude and seek opportunities to share our blessings with others.

Meditation and Prayer Requests

As we meditate on St. Cajetan's life, let us ask for his intercession in the following areas:

A grateful heart

Opportunities for generosity

Wisdom in using our resources

A spirit of sharing

Scripture Reading

1 Thessalonians 5:18 Give thanks in all circumstances; for this is God's will for you in Christ Jesus.

Closing Prayers

Our Father, who art in heaven, hallowed be thy name; thy kingdom come; thy will be done; on earth as it is in heaven. Give us this day our daily bread. And forgive us our trespasses, as we forgive those who trespass against us. And lead us not into temptation, but deliver us from evil. For thine is the kingdom, and the power, and the glory, for ever and ever. Amen.

Hail Mary, full of grace, the Lord is with thee. Blessed art thou amongst women, and blessed is the fruit of thy womb, Jesus. Holy Mary, Mother of God, pray for us sinners, now and at the hour of our death. Amen.

Hail, holy Queen, Mother of mercy, hail, our life, our sweetness and our hope. To thee do we cry, poor banished children of Eve: to thee do we send up our sighs, mourning and weeping in this vale of tears. Turn then, mostgracious Advocate, thine eyes of mercy toward us, and after this our exile, show unto us the blessed fruit of thy womb, Jesus. O clement, O loving, O sweet Virgin Mary! Pray for us, O holy Mother of God, that we may be made worthy of the promises of Christ. Amen.

Glory be to the Father, and to the Son, and to the Holy Spirit. As it was in the beginning, is now, and ever shall be, world without end. Amen.

Prayer for Employment and Overcoming Financial Difficulties

O Saint Cajetan, patron of work and provision, help us cultivate a heart filled with gratitude for the blessings in our lives. Inspire us to share our resources with those in need, recognizing that our possessions are gifts from God. As we strive to overcome financial challenges, grant us the grace to be generous even in difficult times. Amen.

St. Cajetan, pray for us.

In the name of the Father, and of the Son, and of the Holy Spirit. Amen.

Chapter 6

Day 6

Perseverance and Faithfulness

Opening Prayers

In the name of the Father, and of the Son, and of the Holy Spirit. Amen.

Act of Contrition

O my God, I am heartily sorry for having offended You, and I detest all my sins because of Your love for me. I resolve with Your help to confess my sins, to do penance, and to amend my life. Amen.

Theme and Reflection

Today, we focus on the virtues of perseverance and faithfulness. Like St. Cajetan, we are called to persist in prayer and trust in God's providence, even in the face of challenges. Let us renew our commitment to remain steadfast in our faith.

Meditation and Prayer Requests

As we meditate on St. Cajetan's life, let us ask for his intercession in the following areas:

Strength to persevere through difficulties

Faithfulness to God's will

Patience in waiting for God's timing

Courage to overcome obstacles

Scripture Reading

James 1:2-4 Consider it pure joy, my brothers and sisters, whenever you face trials of many kinds, because you know that the testing of your faith produces perseverance. Let perseverance finish itswork so that you may be mature and complete, not lacking anything.

Closing Prayers

Our Father, who art in heaven, hallowed be thy name; thy kingdom come; thy will be done; on earth as it is in heaven. Give us this day our daily bread. And forgive us our trespasses, as we forgive those who trespass against us. And lead us not into temptation, but deliver us from evil. For thine is the kingdom, and the power, and the glory, for ever and ever. Amen.

Hail Mary, full of grace, the Lord is with thee. Blessed art thou amongst women, and blessed is the fruit of thy womb, Jesus. Holy Mary, Mother of God, pray for us sinners, now and at the hour of our death. Amen.

Hail, holy Queen, Mother of mercy, hail, our life, our sweetness and our hope. To thee do we cry, poor banished children of Eve: to thee do we send up our sighs, mourning and weeping in this vale of tears. Turn then, mostgracious Advocate, thine eyes of mercy toward us, and after this our exile, show unto us the blessed fruit of thy womb, Jesus. O clement, O loving, O sweet Virgin Mary! Pray for us, O holy Mother of God, that we may be made worthy of the promises of Christ. Amen.

Glory be to the Father, and to the Son, and to the Holy Spirit. As it was in the beginning, is now, and ever shall be, world without end. Amen.

Prayer for Employment and Overcoming Financial Difficulties

O Saint Cajetan, patron of work and provision, inspire us with your unwavering faith and perseverance. Grant us the strength to endure challenges and the patience to wait for God's timing. Help us to remain faithful to our dreams and goals, even in the face of setbacks. As we seek employment and work to overcome financial difficulties, give us the courage to persevere with hope and trust in your divine providence. Amen.

St. Cajetan, pray for us.

In the name of the Father, and of the Son, and of the Holy Spirit. Amen.

Chapter 7

Day 7

Protection and Peace

Opening Prayers

In the name of the Father, and of the Son, and of the Holy Spirit. Amen.

Act of Contrition

O my God, I am heartily sorry for having offended You, and I detest all my sins because of Your love for me. I resolve with Your help to confess my sins, to do penance, and to amend my life. Amen.

Theme and Reflection

Today, we seek St. Cajetan's intercession for protection and peace. In a world filled with uncertainty, we long for security and tranquility. Let us trust in God's loving care and seek His peace that surpasses understanding.

Meditation and Prayer Requests

As we meditate on St. Cajetan's life, let us ask for his intercession in the following areas:

Protection from harm and danger

Peace of mind and heart

Strength to face challenges with courage

Trust in God's providence

Scripture Reading

Psalm 23:1-4 The Lord is my shepherd, I shall not want. He makes me lie down in green pastures, he leads me beside quiet waters, he restores my soul. He guides me in paths of righteousness for his name's sake.

Closing Prayers

Our Father, who art in heaven, hallowed be thy name; thy kingdom come; thy will be done; on earth as it is in heaven. Give us this day our daily bread. And forgive us our trespasses, as we forgive those who trespass against us. And lead us not into temptation, but deliver us from evil. For thine is the kingdom, and the power, and the glory, for ever and ever. Amen.

Hail Mary, full of grace, the Lord is with thee. Blessed art thou amongst women, and blessed is the fruit of thy womb, Jesus. Holy Mary, Mother of God, pray for us sinners, now and at the hour of our death. Amen.

Hail, holy Queen, Mother of mercy, hail, our life, our sweetness and our hope. To thee do we cry, poor banished children of Eve: to thee do we send up our sighs, mourning and weeping in this vale of tears. Turn then, mostgracious Advocate, thine eyes of mercy toward us, and after this our exile, show unto us the blessed fruit of thy womb, Jesus. O clement, O loving, O sweet Virgin Mary! Pray for us, O holy Mother of God, that we may be made worthy of the promises of Christ. Amen.

Glory be to the Father, and to the Son, and to the Holy Spirit. As it was in the beginning, is now, and ever shall be, world without end. Amen.

Prayer for Employment and Overcoming Financial Difficulties

O Saint Cajetan, patron of work and provision, we turn to you for protection and peace amidst life's challenges. Shield us from harm and grant us serenity of mind and heart. As we face financial difficulties and the uncertainties of employment, help us to trust in God's plan for our lives. May we find peace in knowing that we are cared for by a loving Father. Amen.

St. Cajetan, pray for us.

In the name of the Father, and of the Son, and of the Holy Spirit. Amen.

Chapter 8

Day 8

Hope and Renewal

Opening Prayers

In the name of the Father, and of the Son, and of the Holy Spirit. Amen.

Act of Contrition

O my God, I am heartily sorry for having offended You, and I detest all my sins because of Your love for me. I resolve with Your help to confess my sins, to do penance, and to amend my life. Amen.

Theme and Reflection

Today, we focus on hope and renewal. Even in the midst of challenges, we can find reasons to hope. Let us trust in God's promises and seek His strength to renew our spirits.

Meditation and Prayer Requests

As we meditate on St. Cajetan's life, let us ask for his intercession in the following areas:

A renewed sense of hope

Strength to persevere

Courage to face the future

God's guidance for our path

Scripture Reading

Jeremiah 29:11 "For I know the plans I have for you," declares the Lord, "plans to prosper you and not to harm you, plans to give you hope and a future."

Closing Prayers

Our Father, who art in heaven, hallowed be thy name; thy kingdom come; thy will be done; on earth as it is in heaven. Give us this day our daily bread. And forgive us our trespasses, as we forgive those who trespass against us. And lead us not into temptation, but deliver us from evil. For thine is the kingdom, and the power, and the glory, for ever and ever. Amen.

Hail Mary, full of grace, the Lord is with thee. Blessed art thou amongst women, and blessed is the fruit of thy womb, Jesus. Holy Mary, Mother of God, pray for us sinners, now and at the hour of our death. Amen.

Hail, holy Queen, Mother of mercy, hail, our life, our sweetness and our hope. To thee do we cry, poor banished children of Eve: to thee do we send up our sighs, mourning and weeping in this vale of tears. Turn then, mostgracious Advocate, thine eyes of mercy toward us, and after this our exile, show unto us the blessed fruit of thy womb, Jesus. O clement, O loving, O sweet Virgin Mary! Pray for us, O holy Mother of God, that we may be made worthy of the promises of Christ. Amen.

Glory be to the Father, and to the Son, and to the Holy Spirit. As it was in the beginning, is now, and ever shall be, world without end. Amen.

Prayer for Employment and Overcoming Financial Difficulties

O Saint Cajetan, patron of work and provision, fill our hearts with hope as we face the challenges of employment and finances. Grant us the strength to persevere and the courage to embrace the future with optimism. Help us to trust in God's plan for our lives, knowing that He will provide for our needs. Amen.

St. Cajetan, pray for us.

In the name of the Father, and of the Son, and of the Holy Spirit. Amen.

Chapter 9

Day 9

Consecration to St. Cajetan

Opening Prayers

In the name of the Father, and of the Son, and of the Holy Spirit. Amen.

Act of Contrition

O my God, I am heartily sorry for having offended You, and I detest all my sins because of Your love for me. I resolve with Your help to confess my sins, to do penance, and to amend my life. Amen.

Theme and Reflection

Today, we conclude our novena by consecrating ourselves to St. Cajetan's intercession. Let us renew our commitment to trust in Divine Providence and to seek God's will in all things.

Meditation and Prayer Requests

As we meditate on St. Cajetan's life, let us ask for his continued intercession and guidance:

A deeper relationship with God

Strength to live according to God's plan

A spirit of service to others

The grace to overcome challenges

Scripture Reading

Romans 12:1-2 Therefore, I urge you, brothers and sisters, in view of God's mercy, to offer your bodies as a living sacrifice, holy and pleasing to God—this is your spiritual worship. Do not be conformed to this world, but be transformed by the renewal of your mind, that by testing you may discern what is the will of God, what is good and acceptable and perfect.

Closing Prayers

Our Father, who art in heaven, hallowed be thy name; thy kingdom come; thy will be done; on earth as it is in heaven. Give us this day our daily bread. And forgive us our trespasses, as we forgive those who trespass against us. And lead us not into temptation, but deliver us from evil. For thine is the kingdom, and the power, and the glory, for ever and ever. Amen.

Hail Mary, full of grace, the Lord is with thee. Blessed art thou amongst women, and blessed is the fruit of thy womb, Jesus. Holy Mary, Mother of God, pray for us sinners, now and at the hour of our death. Amen.

Hail, holy Queen, Mother of mercy, hail, our life, our sweetness and our hope. To thee do we cry, poor banished children of Eve: to thee do we send up our sighs, mourning and weeping in this vale of tears. Turn then, mostgracious Advocate, thine eyes of mercy toward us, and after this our exile, show unto us the blessed fruit of thy womb, Jesus. O clement, O loving, O sweet Virgin Mary! Pray for us, O holy Mother of God, that we may be made worthy of the promises of Christ. Amen.

Glory be to the Father, and to the Son, and to the Holy Spirit. As it was in the beginning, is now, and ever shall be, world without end. Amen.

Prayer for Employment and Overcoming Financial Difficulties

O Saint Cajetan, patron of work and provision, we consecrate ourselves to your intercession. We ask for your continued guidance and support as we seek employment and overcome financial challenges. Help us to live in accordance with God's will and to use our resources wisely. May we always trust in Divine Providence and find peace in your loving care. Amen.

St. Cajetan, pray for us.

In the name of the Father, and of the Son, and of the Holy Spirit. Amen.

A Final Blessing

As we conclude this novena to St. Cajetan, may we carry with us a renewed sense of faith, hope, and trust in Divine Providence. Through prayer and reflection, we have deepened our relationship with St. Cajetan and sought his intercession for our needs. Let us continue to invoke his powerful patronage as we navigate the challenges and joys of life.

Encouragement for Continued Prayer

This novena is just the beginning of our spiritual journey. Let us strive to maintain a consistent prayer life, seeking guidance and strength from God through daily meditation and reflection. Continue to turn to St. Cajetan as a faithful intercessor, and share your experiences with others to inspire and uplift them.

May the blessings of God be upon you as you embark on this new chapter of faith and hope.

Printed in Great Britain
by Amazon